Medicine Stone

Medicine Stone

poems

Jack Coulehan (signature)

Jack Coulehan

2002 · FITHIAN PRESS, SANTA BARBARA

Published by Fithian Press
A division of Daniel and Daniel, Publishers, Inc.
Post Office Box 1525
Santa Barbara, CA 93102
www.danielpublishing.com

LIBRARY OF CONGRESS CATALOGING-IN-PUBLICATION DATA
 Coulehan, John L., (date)
  Medicine stone : poems / by Jack Coulehan.
     p. cm.
  ISBN 1-56474-405-1
  1. Medicine—Poetry. 2. Physician and patient—Poetry. 3. Chekhov, Anton
     Pavlovich, 1860–1904—Poetry. 4. Authors—Poetry. I. Title.
  PS3603.O85 M43 2002
  811'.54—dc21
                    2001007918

Once again, for Anne

Some of these poems, or earlier versions of them, first appeared in the following magazines: *Bellevue Literary Review*, "Resources for Life." *The Cape Rock*, "Guam." *Centennial Review*, "Lima Bean." *Cincinnati Poetry Review*, "Harbor Seals." *Prairie Schooner*, "The Six-Hundred-Pound Man." *North Atlantic Review*, "Sunsets." *Potpourri*, "Work Rounds." *Rattle*, "The Origin of Light." *St. Andrews Review*, "Chrysler for Sale." *Trouveré*, "Decatur in Winter."

I am grateful to the *Journal of the American Medical Association* for permission to reprint the following poems: "Amber," "The Anatomist," "The Nervous Breakdown," "Happiness," "The Righteous Shelestov," "Olga Laments the Death of Osip," "Mikhail Ivanovitch Speaks to the Princess," "The Zemstvo Doctor," "Ragin," "Sakhalin Island," "Cholera," "Six Prescriptions," "Chekhov at Yalta," "The Cherry Orchard," "Complications," "Crabs," "D-Day," "House Calls," "Lachrymae Rerun," "Massapequa," "My Machine," "Sirens," "Swimming," "Migraine: A Villanelle," "The Zoo," and "Sonnet for Jack."

I also wish to thank *The Lancet* for permission to reprint "Eunice," "Chekhov Makes Love at a Distance," "The Student," "For Oysters Only," and "The Pounds of Flesh."

"Brain Fever," "Black Bugs," and "Heroes" appeared in *The Journal of Family Practice*. "The Shoe," "I'm Gonna Slap Those Doctors," "I'm Always Grateful for Breakfast," and "The Man with Stars Inside" were published in *The Annals of Internal Medicine*. "Sir William Osler Remembers His Call on Walt Whitman" first appeared in *Journal of Medical Humanities*.

The following poems appeared in *The Knitted Glove* (1991): "Anatomy Lesson," "I'm Gonna Slap Those Doctors," and "The Man with Stars Inside."

"Complications," "Lima Bean," "Sunsets," and "The First Ascent of the Future" are from *First Photographs of Heaven* (1994).

"D-Day, 1994," "House Calls," "The Cherry Orchard," "Cholera," and "Guam" appeared in *The Heavenly Ladder* (2001).

Contents

Medicine Stone

Lachrymae Rerun

Fried flounder on cardboard plates, slaw,
drafts of dark beer. Pain has followed us here
to the fish place in Riverhead. I'm fed up
with clammers' shot backs, bad kidneys,
and their wives' arthritis. I'm fed up
with cancer wearing suspenders and dousing
its flagrant heart in wine. The tables here
are crammed with pain. The coolers
are stacked with eel like black,
pickled sausage. Go ahead, though, keep talking
about your cancer's home—the church
you grew up in, its Baroque Italian priest
and pinched nuns that scuttled across your youth
like bugs. You're not buying it, not an ounce
of original sin, not a word of Augustine,
nor anything that carries you down
from joy. That's what you *say*. Even the walls
of this joint are sweating blood, but you've
converted to a new belief in the cosmic dance.
Go ahead, keep talking. I'm not thinking now
about the sweating bodies of the dead
in Africa, nor that woman with the bomb
beneath her t-shirt in Sri Lanka, nor the kid
gunned down in Brooklyn, nor the arrogance
of righteous violence. I'm trying to imagine
the original blessing. Go ahead, tell me
the wizened eel of history is somebody's fault,
Jesus' or the popes' and if left to ourselves
we'd surely dance. And be compassionate
and tender. Go ahead, finish your beer.
Let's kick up our heels. It's Saturday night
in any case, and I'm tired, too, of tears.

My Machine

If I had a machine to use
in a case like yours, I'd use it
on the nucleus that makes
my feelings, to deepen them.

I'd take a long time, like a monk
at morning prayer, before I spoke
and turned each word into a sign
of passion. When I told you,

yes, the damage is more
than anyone knew, I'd hold you
in my arms, desperately close
like death. I'd throw off the sham

of working in a reasoned way
to find the answers to your pain.
Instead, I'd use an archaic
neural poem and feel the pull

of healing, skin to skin, instead of
acting neither man nor woman
and doing the decent thing. The ache
would be a price worth paying.

Anatomy Lesson

When I move your body
from its storage drawer,
I brush my knuckles,
Ernest, on your three-days
growth of beard. Cheeks,
wet with formaldehyde,
prickle with cactus.
My eyes burn and blink
as if a wind of sand
blew through the room.

Bless me, Ernest,
for I cut your skin
to learn positions
and connections
of your parts—caves,
canyons, fissures, faults,
all of you. Show me.
Show me your flowers,
your minerals, the oil
of your spleen.

Do not mistake these tears.
These tears are not
for your bad luck
nor my indenture here,
but for all offenses
to the heart—yours, mine—
for the violence
of abomination.
Think of my tears as rain
staining your canyon walls,
filling your stream,
touching the blossoms.

Complications

The last time Nate came in
he smelled like Grace did when
she worked door-to-door
for Avon. He had the one
pierced earring in, his beard
was trimmed, he had the cane
with a devil's head, the one
Grace used to clobber him
the night she stroked. The last time
Nate came in, the housing cops
had been—they took his two
big dogs. And then he was
alone. No matter what he did
the kids would bust his locks
and trash the place.

Nate found a woman half his age
or she found him. He wound up
in Baltimore, drunk, without
a bank account and by himself.
When he made it home
both guns were gone. Then Nate
was put in jail for D & D
a time or two. At the end
they phoned me from the morgue—
in his pants the boys
had found an old appointment card

and Nate's
Certificate of Satisfactory Service,
nothing else. They asked
if I would sign him out
and save the boys a trip?
I said, sure, *Let's give the man
a heart attack.* Then I thought
of Grace's stroke, only I
didn't say a word about Grace,
just, *Boys, the cause of death
was complications.*

Brain Fever

reminds me of Sarah Gorecki
propped-up in bed, fluffed pillows
along her sides and her husband
in his chair by the black window
doing the day's crossword. She took
to bed the week they shut the mill
in Donora, which is exactly
how George remembers it

coming home with his last check
already bit by a few drinks,
he found her under the comforter
whispering how cold she was.
What fits she had! One spell led
to another—red pills, the big
green pills, the gallbladder. At last
the neighbors stopped pestering her
and telling her she's getting stronger.

Sarah told me the brain fever
set in that summer like coffin fog
on a damp day by the river. It spread
deep behind her eyes and made her weaker
than a pigeon. George was a real
lifesaver, though. After thirty years
of staying out and of cutting-up,
that man sure came down in a hurry.

The Cock

"Crito, I owe a cock to Asclepius."
—Socrates' last words

Remember the guy who left his doctor's office
with a clean bill of health? Next thing you know
he's in intensive care, he dropped dead in
the parking lot, thank God for mouth-to-mouth.

For a long time nobody knew where he was
but he shows up in Santa Fe, where he works
in a bicycle shop and takes long walks
in the mountains. He wants me to tell you

it's okay on the other side, he's not afraid,
he'll never be afraid again, he's writing
a book about it. He wants me to tell you
it doesn't matter, he puts a hand on his heart

and swears it doesn't matter. He's leaner now
than when he used to ride the 6:45
the whole year around and wear his overcoat,
although the sun has broken down his skin.

He kids about the cock of gratitude
he owes to some guy named Asclepius
who must be a doc, I guess, and makes me
promise, when I go back, to wring one's neck

and offer it to Asclepius for him.
He always was a card, that guy, you can't tell
when he's serious. The way he lived,
something strange was bound to happen and it did.

Eunice

We've been trying to get you all night, doctor,
came the voice in the phone that was, like,
the only word I can think of is *furtive*,
and angry, too, in a way, but hovering
at nearly sheepishness. I'm stewing around
in the few unbroken vistas that were left
of a dream, which had a moment ago
been jetting an airboat up the Knik River
in Alaska, and then this voice comes, *We've
been trying to get you*, as if I've never had
a trying moment myself, and there might be
dozens of them, scores of faceless men out there
scouring the morning like Mussolini's
Brown Shirts, rampaging the deserted streets
in search of me, or a hive of chitinous jaws
and clenched wings on their way to my house.
We think she's taken a turn, she's definitely
taken a turn, my sister says, and we think she's,
or she might have been, asking for you. *But
I'm not on call today*—the only punch
I could think of, which I kept hitting him with
again and again, each time more desperately,
but he feinted each punch, or absorbed it,
and said, But, doctor, remember the oath,
remember the solemn oath that you promised,
what about it, you know, until death do us part,

remember how much you once meant to her,
you're the old doctor, the one she used to go to
before she got so sick and needed
a specialist. My sister says her eyes are, like,
turned back, so that the white, you know, is all
you see except for a little scoop at the top
and we can't tell whether she's breathing or not.
If you ask me, it doesn't look like she is,
it looks, I wouldn't want to say this too loud,
it looks like she's dead, but you know my sister,
how delicate she is, and, God forbid,
I wouldn't want her to think that it's too late
and there's no hope for Eunice. There's always hope.

House Calls

After they took her lung out for cancer,
the progress was quiet. First, she resigned

as queen of the most expensive club
on the island. Then she ensconced herself

in the room that was once her father's
sancta sanctorum. From his overstuffed chair

she wheedled the nurses into mixing
an endless succession of martinis.

She never left the house except to see
the eye doctor, and never ate a bite

without complaint. The fiction they picked
to explain her eccentricity

was fear of cancer, but it was more like
a day without drink that frightened her.

When I inquired about the vitamins,
she didn't need them. When I took a look

at her throat, her coquetry came back.
She asked if I could sniff her little drink?

When I listened to the raucous moisture
in her chest, she told me that her doctor

her *real* doctor was promoted to professor
and *left me like you all do.*

When she didn't die that first year, her brother
flew in to check my credentials.

He was a lint-free man if I ever met one,
silver-haired and chairman of the board,

but I spoke too softly to charm him
and my car was embarrassing.

The last straw was me visiting her house.
I must be angling for a piece

of her will, or at least a better job.
When he returned to St. Thomas,

I was sent back to the minors.
So much for my money-practice

that had never amounted to much
she didn't carry a stitch

of insurance and wasn't the type
to bother with details like paying the help.

Heroes

You call them *scuzballs*
when they roll in
at midnight, seizing,
with lavender silk shirts
covering their cruddy chests.

But remember the myth among them—

they are sons and daughters
of dukes, the heirs of dukes,
and deserving of love,

they are the lost children
of heroes, the bastard
progeny of gods,

remember their hearts
are the hearts of heroes,

and when you place the stethoscope,

ride the palm of your right hand
along their galloping steeds
and listen.

I'm Gonna Slap Those Doctors

Because the rosy condition
makes my nose bumpy and big,
and I give them the crap they deserve,
they write me off as a boozer
and snow me with drugs. Like I'm gonna
go wild and green bugs are gonna
crawl on me and I'm gonna tear out
their goddamn precious IV.
I haven't had a drink in a year
but those slick bastards cross their arms
and talk about sodium. They come
with their noses crunched up like my room
is purgatory and they're the
goddamn angels doing a bit
of social work. Listen, I might not
have much of a body left,
but I've got good arms — the polio
left me that — and the skin on my hands
is about an inch thick. And when I used
to drink I could hit with the best
in Braddock. Listen, one more shot
of the crap that makes my tongue stop
and they'll have something on their hands
they didn't know existed. They'll have time
on their hands. They'll be spinning around
drunk as skunks, heads screwed on backwards,
and then Doctor Big Nose is gonna smell
their breaths, wrinkle his forehead, and spin
down the hall in his wheelchair
on the way to the goddamn heavenly choir.

Massapequa

What can you do but stand and complain,
the way things are going? Take the sins
of that unspeakable man, take the shame
and banishment, take years of bitterness
in Massapequa. And then you learn
he's been saved by a preacher in Delaware,
which makes it worse—guiltless! The way
life is these days, the bad don't suffer,
nor the just inherit. The women
are loose. And guilt is a thing of the past.

What can you do when you're stranded
in this hard, brazen country, in a room
on the second floor, when all about you
is music and swearing? You want to talk
about your dream of becoming a nurse,
but the words don't follow. They keep
returning to the night it all began,
when he forced your door and stayed.

That's what led to the disease. Everything
has followed since. Like a caged canary
in a gaseous mine, you died of the first breath.
You never believed that penicillin
made you clean, but you kept working on
cleanliness and collecting novenas.
Yea, sure, he married a tart in Delaware,
he hasn't touched a drink of booze in years.
But where's the justice? What can you do
about the past, but cry your eyes out?

The Pounds of Flesh

You weighed one hundred five the day
you married. It's been a battle since—
buttocks, abs—but you held fast until this.

You swat the child's hands from your hoops
and gold chain. Droolingly, he makes you
wipe your blouse and failed thighs with juice

and your weightlessness hoists the burden
of gravity. *The pounds will disappear
in time,* I explain. If only she had faith

in natural law, Aquinas could show,
within a pound or two, her weight just fits,
but she has no faith in him, and I'm alone.

I want to say, Your orange scent is attractive,
as are your large breasts, no matter what size
your husband desires. Appearances are

deceiving, even when you can't see them.
I'm sure the weight will suddenly fade,
like all we prize in life, but I can't say when.

Home, Sweet Home

Thirty-seven times. No wonder my hands look
as deeply scored as a satellite shot
of canyons in Utah—take that image
as characteristic of me, different
but not stupid. I'm no half-baked child kept home
for lack of sense, whose face is structured wrong.

My penchant for washing my hands is a wrong
connection that feels right. Yes, if I look
at myself from your perspective—at home
wasting time—I'm queerer than they come. Your shot
of me scrubbing my hands like a differently
gendered Lady Macbeth, an image

that evokes a shutter of guilt, is an image
that doesn't do me justice. You'd be wrong
to sic the dogs of sense on my different
tics and habits and insist on looking
at the reasons an achiever like me has shot
his own foot and decided to stay home

instead of breaking out. Well, "Home, Sweet Home"
is a good song. After my wife's image
spun down the drain, my nerves were shot
and my heart shuddered, but it would be wrong
to say the hurt came first, or that I looked
into the mirror thirty-seven different

times a day, scrubbing my hands with different
lotions and creams and singing "Home, Sweet Home"
each time on account of the past looking
like it victimized me. Your image
of a child screwing up the machine is wrong,
wrong, wrong! My life felt good until they shot

me down and made me anxious, and I shot
my wad explaining how I was different
from others, and even if it was wrong
for my skin (poor thing!), I'd best stay home
and scrub my hands, rather than imagine
myself otherwise (on drugs) with the same look

the others have, *your* look, not by a long shot
a liberated image, just a different
kind of coercion. No, I'm not wrong to stay home.

The Storm

When you stop at the home
to visit, my friend said,
it's a toss-up—she might be good
that day, or bad. It's tragic
the way her mind fades, she's out
for a smoke. There's nothing
inside.
       I should have known
her silence couldn't keep
forever. Sooner or later
she'd have to expose herself
to the insult of being
remembered by students
and children. But whose pain
am I dishing out? I ought
to be grateful the storm
that might have dumped a foot
of snow on us will pass
upstate, another near miss
for the Island, like a thought
pushed aside when a thick,
dark mass moves in and begins
to smother the brain and slow
its time until it grinds,
timeless, to a stop. I see her
tamping a plug of tobacco,

lighting her cob pipe—the first
woman I met who smoked
like a man—and leaning back
behind her desk, a brilliantly
tough-minded talker. Scary, too,
for a young man with a weak
sense of what it would mean
to stand up. Where is she?
Locked in? Broken down? What
a waste this weather is!
After the hype all week
on the News and the frenzy
of romance, it seems we're back
to the old routine again,
saved from that hundred-year storm.

Death House

Each day your cluttered bed
reveals a different version
of the house you're making
of cardboard, balsa wood,
and the Popsicle sticks
your sister brought, a design
you sketched, but abandoned,
a dozen years back
because your wife had split
by then, and you were broke.
The house is crisp, every bit
as fine as those you built
for the rich in Southampton,
those eccentric retreats
erected for delight.
It's even better, you explain,
brushing a few slivers
of gluey debris
from your distended abdomen's
shelf, and showing me
the latest improvement
on your old design. Today's touch
is a railing for the porch.
Yesterday's—a larger deck.
Last week you made a ramp
from the children's bedroom
to the pool. But tonight
you'll tear that feature out,

or add a window, or re-size
the molding, so when I come
again tomorrow morning
to talk about dying,
the house, like Penelope's shroud,
will be no closer
to completion, and you'll look
at the pile of cardboard and glue
on your table and tell me
you need more time. It's such a job
getting everything to fit
and you have to be patient.

Medicine Stone

This stone I picked at a medicine dance
on a cold June day near Wounded Knee.

In my bare feet, I carried this stone
into the circle of those with need.

A sun dancer danced in front of me,
touched my shoulder with a sprig of sage.

A sun dancer chanted in front of me
and blessed me with his medicine pipe.

Here in the city, the sky is brilliant.
I carry this stone in a buckskin pouch.

Here in the city, we suffer in private.
Each of us stands at the circle alone.

This stone is an aspect of soul that lasts.
This stone is a remnant of no account.

Here in the hospital, coyote is dead.
This small stone is of no account.

Wolves, spiders, moles, snakes, ants are dead.
This spherical stone is of no account.

Eagles, hummingbirds, ravens, bats are dead.
This stone is a remnant of no account.

Only the voices of suffering live,
the skin, and what happens beneath the skin.

Still, I carry this buckskin pouch
and a small stone wrapped in a wad of sage.

This stone is an aspect of soul that lasts.
I call it my friend, my black stone friend.

The Farmer's Daughter

1946. Night. The young man
who conquered a continent
has returned to the coast of France
to bring back his prize.

Answering the call of nature,
he bundles his clothes
against Normandy's winter
and walks to the privy.

There he is, a miner's son
from Pittsburgh, looking
for all the world, and finding it
in the farmer's daughter.

What a night this is!
The farm she sang about
last year in Paris, wine,
cigars, and an evening of relatives.

Tomorrow, the train
for America leaves. To him,
now, almost anything
is possible—a lusty

French bride, her immaculate
skin, the gift of a job
at Jerry's Hardware, the chance
for a correspondence course.

He relieves himself
into that cold, black circle
before him, his steaming piss
marks his place in history—

as the man who survives
for fifty years, who buries
his wife after a long
sickness, whose daughter

leaves, who ushers
for the Church, who never
cries, or sets his failing eyes
again on France.

D-Day, 1994

Your arm is gone
to cancer at 30—no honor
in that. The potato-like stump
is not where the pain is.

You take your pills
and watch TV—
where beaches in France
swim with images of old men
pacing the coast for the first time
since going down.

You notice their limps
and imagine the vacancies—
fear, lost limbs, their buddies dead.
Who would have thought
the first tide of grunts
attacking that fortified coast
could win the war?

You ask if a scan would explain
the pain in your phantom limb,
believing a scan is like a story
that reveals things. Those men
creeping the grey-crossed breast
of a hill on the coast of France—
they know what they lost, they know
what they are looking for.

The scan will not give you an answer.
You are looking in the wrong place
for an answer. The world works hard
to hide its d-day—
deception, danger, death,
deliverance. I wish I could give you
the old men's stories. I wish I could give you
their battles, which are almost used up
but still true.

The Man With Stars Inside

Deep in this old man's chest,
a shadow of pneumonia grows.
I watch Antonio shake
with a cough that traveled here
from the beginning of life.
As he pulls my hand to his lips
and kisses my hand,
Antonio tells me
for a man whose death
is gnawing at his spine,
pneumonia is a welcome friend,
a friend who reaches
deep between his ribs without a sound
and puff! a cloud begins to squeeze
so delicately
the great white image of his heart.

The shadow on his X-ray grows
each time Antonio moves,
each time a nurse
smoothes lotion on his back
or puts a fleece between his limbs.
Each time he takes a sip of ice
and his moist chest shakes with cough,
the shadow grows.

In that delicate shadow
is a cloud of gas
at the galaxy's center,
a cloud of cold stunned nuclei
beginning to spin,
spinning and shooting
a hundred thousand embryos of stars.
I listen to Antonio's chest
where stars crackle from the past,
and hear the boom
of blue giants, newly caught,
and the snap of white dwarfs
coughing, spinning.
The second time
Antonio kisses my hand
I feel his dusky lips
reach out from everywhere in space.
I look at the place
his body was,
and see inside, the stars.

I'm Always Grateful for Breakfast

The frail woman who struggles with the seat
beside mine puts a plate of cantaloupe
at her place, nodding slightly before she retreats

to the buffet and returns with a second plate
of cantaloupe, the coincidence of which
darkens her face in amazement. Look at that!

Two plates! She chuckles at happenstance,
but in her face impenetrable damage
stays fast. Why must her imagination slip?

What prison does her mind inhabit?
Her rheumy eyes are apricot pits
on a plate of water. Her pearls are seeds

in barren soil. As I pull back the chair for her,
she confesses in a mixture of kindness
and terror, "I'm always grateful for breakfast."

Sirens

"What song the Syrens sang…(is) not beyond all conjecture."
—*Thomas Browne (1605–1682)*

Their song is a generous wind
from the island's throat. Listen,
my friend. You must learn to forget
the violence you're accustomed to
and years of hapless voyage.

At first you can't imagine
a respite from discipline,
from the petulant telephone
telling its worst—of intractable
pain, unthinkable dread.

A respite from Alfred,
who never met the therapist
you sent him to, not once.
From all the petty coughs
and silent screams.

From Richard's desperate chest—
he's lost his job, his energy,
his hope. He doesn't know
where his misfortune comes from,
but knows you'll make it go.

Your heart has claims of its own,
the Sirens sing. Abandon
discipline. Your body can't take
the knots it's tied in. Come closer,
we'll loosen them.

The Shoe

Public Health Inspector William Townsend,
died 1968, Black River, Jamaica

Townsend took a curve too fast
and died near the coast. Nobody heard
for hours. Every few minutes
I turned to the window and cursed him.
He won't come, I thought, *the bastard won't.*

The road from Magotty came up
the curves of banana trees battered by rain,
but the sick arrived anyway.
Glistening loudly, they filled the clinic.
We walked up and down to quiet their babies.

I was witless with anger.
Townsend had promised to come at noon
and take us away—we had such
important work to do. *Americans!*
Sister clicked her teeth at my arrogance.

At Townsend's funeral, his father
held up a shoe and cried, *He walked
in the pathways of righteousness.* I sat,
rod straight, on a folding chair
at the front of the church and didn't speak.

For isn't righteousness the brother
I never had? In Babylon,
years later, I listen for the sound
of Townsend's shoes. In play, he'll punch
my shoulder. I'll follow him anywhere.

Work Rounds: On Lines by Tomas Transtromer

The lessons of official life
go rumbling on.
We send inspired notes
to one another.

The parade of distracted figures slows,
eddies, and each slides an "s"
around the obstruction—a lorry
of breakfasts and a medicine cart.

I am looking at you, at the fringe of hair
you didn't pull tight. A shaft of sun
pierces the mountainous clouds in your eyes.
You must be bursting with news.

Has the man in the next room returned at last
from his journeying fever? Has he sent us
a message? You look to the chart
and show me, *This is the culture. Negative.*

All these years I, too, have hoped for the same thing—
an inspired note. Listen, I am grateful
for the gift of your news. How unlikely
his improvement was! And for the messenger's grace.

The Six-Hundred-Pound Man

Of the six-hundred-pound man on two beds,
nothing remains,
not the bleariness with which he moved his eyes
nor the warm oil curling in his beard.

Though the sheets and plastic bags are gone,
his grunts, his kind acceptance gone,
I see him now, rising in the distance,
an island, mountainous
and hooded with impenetrable vine.

When I awaken to the death
of the six-hundred-pound man
and cannot sleep again,
I paddle to his shore

in search of those flamboyant trees
that flame his flanks,
in search of bougainvillea
blossoming his thighs,
of women who rise to touch him
tenderly with ointment,

in search of healers, singers
who wrestle souls of old bodies
back to bones, back to dirt, and back back
to their beginnings.

As I enter for the first time
this medicine circle,
bearing chickens in honor of the god,
words dancing from my lips,

spirit like the plume of a child's volcano
rises

and then the medicine, the medicine is good
and the tongues, the tongues are dancing
and the fathers, oh! the fathers are dancing

and this worthless and alien body,
this six-hundred-pound man,
I discover him beautiful.

The Cherry Orchard

NOTE

After the young Dr. Anton Chekhov achieved early success as a writer, his editor advised him to give up medical practice, arguing that medical work took up valuable time that could be much better used for writing. Chekhov answered, "Medicine is my lawful wedded wife, and literature my mistress. When one gets on my nerves, I spend the night with the other. This may be somewhat disorganized, but then again it's not boring, and anyway neither loses anything by my duplicity." (Letter to Suvorin, 11 September 1888) Chekhov continued to frequent the separate bedrooms of medicine and literature until advanced tuberculosis severely limited his activities.

The poems in this section celebrate the unlikely compatibility between Chekhov's metaphorical wife and mistress. Ten of the poems are based on stories or, in one case, a play. In most of these the central character is a physician. While I hope the reader unfamiliar with the stories will still be able to enjoy the poems, knowing the stories is definitely a big plus. The derivations are: "The Anatomist," *Anyuta*; "The Righteous Shelestov," *Intrigues*; "Olga Laments the Death of Osip," *The Grasshopper*; "Ragin," *Ward #6*; "The Zemstvo Doctor," *Darkness*; "Mikhail Ivanovitch Speaks to the Princess," *The Princess*; and "The Nervous Breakdown," "Happiness," "The Student," and "The Cherry Orchard" borrow the names of the stories that inspired them.

The rest of the poems reflect various incidents in, or aspects of, Chekhov's own life, including his public health work ("Sakhalin Island" and "Cholera"), his medical practice ("Six Prescriptions"), his rather ill-fated pet mongoose ("Mongoose"), his pattern of behavior toward women ("Chekhov's Secret"), his eventual marriage to the actress Olga Knipper ("Chekhov Makes Love at a Distance"), and his terminal illness and death from tuberculosis ("Chekhov at Yalta" and "For Oysters Only").

The Anatomist

Take off your blouse, Anyuta,
and let me examine your bones.
Hold up your arms and I'll trace
the arcs of your scrawny ribs
with my crayon. Your chest
is like a piano's keys—
too damn thin. Be a good girl
and stop that shivering.

Run over to Fedisov's place,
Anyuta, and take your clothes off.
He's in need of a nude for his
classical painting. His model
was no damn good—she had blue legs
from cheap stockings. Couldn't keep
his mind in check, but it's a waste
to talk about that. Get going.

Look, you're slovenly and plain
which matches the rest of my
miserable life. Put on your coat.
We'll have to part in any case,
so why not now? Look at you,
your face quivering with tears,
your lips parted in thought. I can't
concentrate. Stop... stay a week.

The Nervous Breakdown

It's one of those winter nights
when every time you stop
a drink of vodka grabs you
and takes you closer to tears.
That's why I sing to my friends
on our way to visit the whores.
Romantic Vassilyev holds back,
muttering about the circumstance
that brings girls here—their poverty,
the grimness of their peasant life,
the strangling city, his pangs
of social conscience. He has yet
to fathom the world beyond his books—
or to learn the harlots' lingerie
he keeps flicking his eyes from
is not just a mistake of bad taste,
but has a definite purpose.
Vassilyev sits close to the wall
of a purple salon, patiently
asking his whore, *how did you come
here? what is the meaning of this?*
He is startled by her blank
inanimate stare as she asks him
to buy her a drink. What blinders
the man has! He thinks that vice
is attractive only when it wears
the mask of virtue. If I had
the money to take him a step

beyond his grandmotherly
scruples, he'd soon see that lust
contributes more to man's life
than baring the soul. Vassilyev,
my friend, they have a hundred
thousand whores in London—
ten times the whores we have
in Moscow. That's my perspective.
You'd think a dose of reality
would help Vassilyev get himself
together, but he is weak-kneed.
The whores laid him out—in bed,
where he gnashes and weeps for days
at a time. What sort of a friend
is this? *They are alive!* he sobs,
My God, those women are alive!

Happiness

I walk through the meadow—my boots glisten
from the morning's rain—deep in this land
is a trace of the numinous.

A fragrance—the rain has released the fragrance
of grass—some days
I am detached like a stone out of place
but today my heart is enormous.

Today the meadow blazes with wormwood
and tiny bright flowers. Today I recall the tales
of incredible riches, of buried treasure.

Ghost-ridden peasants went to their graves
in search of a map, a key—*if only* was welded to their breasts,
a part of their lives,
what if I found it was their shadow, their bread.

What if I found it lives in me, too—
a monotonous cricket
in the moist steppe of my experience.
It blunts my ears, my soul.

What if I found it makes my attention move elsewhere—
when the cricket chirps
I am unable to feel the movements of my heart—
Today the cricket is silent.

Where will I search for the buried treasure? Where will I dig
for my casket of happiness?
I'll dig right here.

The Righteous Shelestov

I'm spending time in front of the mirror
trying to give my face a languid look—
the look of easy disregard a man
of my importance has—and surely not
an air of nerves. I see it now—my colleagues
squabbling among themselves about my guilt,
tossing around malfeasance-talk,
and demanding my account. *My friends*,
I tell them—with eyes half-bored, my whiskers
languid—*Let he who is without fault*
cast the first point. And then I toss them
line and verse about their skill—take Bronn,
who pierced an esophagus with his probe,
or Zhila who mistook a floating kidney
for infection. *Let me assure you, gentlemen,*
ethics is not the exclusive right
of this Association. After they applaud
my moral power and candor, they censure
my opponents and condemn them.
In a tumult of acclamation
they elect me Chief of the Association!

I notice in the mirror my face is sour
instead of languid, and it appears
dog-like, narrow and desperate, which is not
the noble mien I had in mind. The truth is
they must have lured my face into their camp.
There is no escaping it, my colleagues'
intrigues have gotten out of hand. I puff my cheeks—
there, doesn't that look better? No,
it doesn't. My canine eyes flit back and forth.
Steady, Shelestov, keep your nerve.

Olga Laments the Death of Osip

O good, pure, loving spirit,
why have I let you slip from my life
and abandon the world?

While you spent your unwavering days
with the sick, I stood on the deck
of a Volga steamer. I cuddled in love—

with Ryabovsky, the genius,
who buried his sensitive eyes in my bosom
and let loose his weariness.

We laughed about you; I made up a song—
For a simple person like him,
the happiness he has already had is enough.

When at last I returned, you embraced me.
What a spineless and ordinary man
you were, to torture me with kindness!

I wrapped the shame of our marriage
like a shawl on my shoulders
and wore it that night to Ryabovsky's flat.

How was I to know in your despair
you'd suck seeds of diphtheria
from the throat of a dying patient?

Now, as you lie, so unpleasantly gray,
on my Turkish divan, I see
that indeed you were an unusual man,

bound for celebrity. My strength of soul,
I want to explain my mistake.
If only I had understood. Why didn't you tell me?

Ragin

Wherever I look, the world
is dense with lack. Ignorant towns.
Small tasks. The withering
absence of progressive thought.

The world is jaggedly obscene
with injustice—
the patients in the wards
are prisoners, the prisoners

in the jail are sick. The front
you wear—a toss of luck.
The sickening stench of things
creeps into my appointed rounds

of pacing, beer, and books.
Routine doesn't give me the solace
it once did, and loneliness
drives me to lunatics

for solace. The passion I spent
in youth, which was little enough,
is gone, but the craziness
of passion has come back and knocked me

into visiting the locked ward,
where Gromov abuses me
with his barbed wit. I have yet
to experience suffering,

but I want to. To the watchman
who carries the key,
the difference between Gromov
and me is illusory.

The Zemstvo Doctor

A hell of a thing! His tattered overcoat and red cheeks
remind me of the last petitioner who stood
on the steps of my office. *Please, your honor, help me.*

This time it's his brother in jail. He wants me to plead
his case—the man was drunk and didn't know
what he was doing when he broke into the bakery

and caused such damage. The last time—a different face
blocked my sight, asked me to help him find justice.
He lost his job through no fault of his own and got sick.

What right have I to relieve a drunk of his mean deeds?
Or point my finger at the world and ask for justice?
These petitioners—they come out of the darkness

that surrounds us. Like children they run up to your legs
with open hearts. *To whom shall I go?* they mutter.
Yes, it's true—I want to be known for my compassion

and to walk light on my feet, bearing the gratitude
of men. But I don't know how to respond.
What I *do* know—the world of potions, of bandages—

is of little use to them. It seems the world is worse
each day. I am so sick of this—I wave my hand
in despair and push the man aside and close my door.

Mikhail Ivanovitch Speaks to the Princess

You ask why my eyes
on your famous face
are cold and my words polite,
and why I fail to cherish
your presence, or grovel
at your feet. You ask if I wield
a secret knife to slash
the bones of your mistakes...

If I could open the belly
of your estates, I would expose
the purulence, the hatred,
the agony, you arrogant bitch
of a princess. You raise a finger—
your servants go hungry.
You glance at the sleeve
of your frilled dress—your stooge
takes a dozen families to court.
But here in the monastery,
you lick the abbot's toes
and sleep in a simple cell—
how refreshingly spiritual!

But pardon me, my princess—
when I open my mouth
in your presence, this venom
comes tumbling out, I can't
help it. Too bad for my wallet.
And for your servants, too. Had I stuck
to the business of doctoring
instead of telling the truth, I'd still
be patting my belly at the foot
of your table and treating their ills.

Sakhalin Island

When I entered the hut
and tried to speak to the boy
he winced with his shoulders
and backed away.

The hut smelled, the boy
was barefoot,
scrawny, sodden, and the rain,
demonic.

When I asked about his father
he said, *I don't know my father.*
I'm a bastard.

I could hardly hear his voice
in the violent wind—
it drove wedges of rain
through kinks in the hut's walls.

The boy said his mother was sent
to Sakhalin Island
because of her husband.
My mother's a widow, he explained.

She killed him.

Cholera
Melikhovo, 1892

The epidemic bursts from Astrakhan
and roars north, pushing flames of panic
in front of it. They say the corpse's
muscles can twitch for hours after death,
and peasants whisper, the dead still speak.

Priests take to the road with their icons.
They pester their saints for forgiveness.
A crowd of ruffians enters the room
we've gathered the drugs in and smashes
the bottles. You wouldn't believe their stories.

They say doctors are causing the outbreak—
it's a scheme to keep the population down.
They say big government is behind
the conspiracy—we who work in the field
are dupes, we are the tools of perdition.

Cholera seems to strike for no reason—
it hits the vigorous, the young spill their guts.
The peasants place their bets on evil—
the doctors' or the czar's—as the source of it.
How can they face life if death is meaningless?

They run to the clinic, bludgeon the doors,
chase out the sick. *Escape from the death house!*
There is enough truth in their ignorance
to make you wonder, enough calamity
in their passion to deepen the burden.

Mongoose

Here lies the mongoose that I carried across the world
by steamship from the steamy woodlands of Ceylon
to the breathless, frozen forests south of Moscow.

In the summer my guests cooed when they saw the mongoose
popping his head from our picnic basket. The creature
was a real show-stopper. The lazed twitch of his whiskers

and pointed nose delighted them all, and his bushy tail
could write such unexpected endings, like last week
in the woods—the mongoose bit off a piece of mama's nose

while she crawled around on her knees collecting mushrooms.
No feigned affection there. No holding back or holding forth.
Indeed, the mongoose was a trick of the universe,

a quick correction to easy assumptions. The trickster
could worry a cobra, but if you left him in a room
alone, he'd whimper for hours. May the mongoose rest in peace.

Six Prescriptions

1.

If you talk too much
the blood will rush to your lungs
and deprive the brain,
so don't chatter
and avoid getting constipated.

2.

If you are afraid of stressful living
turn yourself into a smelt or sturgeon.

If you don't want Russia to blow up like Sodom,
go to Kiev for the Easter procession.

If you are fed up with so much suffering,
potassium iodide is a splendid thing.

3.

The doctor I work with
is quiet and homely.
We nearly always disagree.
I give good tidings
where she imagines death
and when she prescribes a dose
I double it.

4.

Don't let her have porridge,
sunflower seeds, or bread.
If she asks for vodka,
give her a cigarette.

Don't improvise
unless you think about it.

5.

Some are for arrowroot.
Some are against.
Others have no strong feelings
either way.

As soon as the bowels become loose,
abandon it.

6.

I grow weary of peasant women
and tired of iodoform.
A girl with worms in her ear,
a monk with syphilis, an opinion
about the nature of illness,
the tedious powders. Phooey!

Oh, sweet sounds of poesy,
where are you?
Come, climb through my window.

The Student

When the student went out to walk at dawn
the weather was fresh, but upon his return
at sunset, shards of ice had started to form
at the pond's edge. The gawky student

burned in a cold wind. Didn't winter's grip,
he asked his interior friend,
squeeze harder each year, like government?
He came to a bonfire near the river

where two women lingered, widows who lived
on cabbage from their garden. The daughter
had been crushed by her husband until her eyes
were vacant. The mother, chilled as well,

had a curious smile that rose from her throat.
Warming his hands at the fire, the student
told them of Peter, who was so afraid
when put to the test that he denied his friend—

not once, but three times. *On a night like this,*
the boy whispered. The old woman's face
crumpled. Her daughter's cheekbones flushed
as if she were blessed with joy, but pierced

at the same moment. *He went out and wept
bitterly.* The boy's mind's entrapment cleared.
He saw himself and the two widows,
and Peter, too, and the crackling fire,

as inexplicably one. He climbed the hill
toward home. It seemed to him that a shaft
from the collapsing purple sun
on the ridge slid across his face and passed.

The Cherry Orchard

"If a great many remedies are suggested for some disease,
it means the disease is incurable."
      —*The Cherry Orchard*

The end of the century
has come upon us
without a sign of release
or the beginning of justice.
We're selling the orchard
to pay our debts
and reminiscing about
love's excitements,
life's mistakes. I suspect
a century ago the hearts
of the people sitting here
were just as generous,
intense, and cruel as ours.

A miniature flower
thrives in the moisture
and dust of a broken
pavement—this is the gist
of the matter. We want
so strongly to believe
the flower will spread
everywhere. How quickly
it dies! If the disease
had a cure, we would not need
so many remedies.

Chekhov Makes Love at a Distance

Sweet marvelous actress,
I bow down before you,
so low that my forehead
scrapes the dry bottom
of the well in my heart—
as a result of your absence
this well is fifty-six feet deep.

My pigeon, you write me
what the weather is like
in Moscow, but I can read
the papers for weather.
My room and my bed
are like a summer cottage,
abandoned. Are not
both of us incomplete?
I'm weary without you.

My sweet dog, last page
of my life, I'm torn up
by the roots, but the body
won't move. I'm hoping
my health holds—you don't
need a seedy old
grandfather in your bed.
O, how I envy the rat
that lives beneath the floor
of your theater!

Chekhov at Yalta

Being sick is repulsive. We talk
about nothing but borsch at Yalta
and there isn't a book to be had.

What an embarrassing situation!
I must remember to walk slowly,
to eat without fail at a proper hour,

to marshal my words to come softly
so they calm my defeated throat.
Being sick is a repulsive dream—

Chekhov, the infamous scribbler,
in his underwear with strangers.
I can't sit down, I can't think straight.

And my discipline has gone to hell.
Fire! What an appropriate image
for days of coughing blood, a small,

but persistent, trickle. No wonder
my tubercular physician
pays attention—he places a mirror

in front of my face, to reflect
the excuses, to diminish
distance between me and my death.

For the public—I cough discreetly
into a paper cone and continue
to talk—no, nothing has happened.

Chekhov's Secret
for Richard Selzer

Regarding his behavior toward women—
Chekhov kept his distance. He rarely
avoided a chance to converse with them,
or even to flirt, but notice the lack
of love affairs in that passionate life—
the itch to keep going, to write, to tell
the truth without varnishing it, to get
the job done, to overcome his father's
failure, but all the while his peculiar
detachment, his diffidence when it came
to romance.
    At a vegetarian shop
in New Haven, a famous surgeon
told me his theory—an anatomical
problem (a small penis, for example)
or ejaculatio praecox
kept Chekhov from women. Until, of course,
consumption made an old man of him
before his time. Even with Olga,
my friend said, *They lived apart. There's no proof*
they consummated. Seeing her miscarriage
in my eyes, he replied, *How do we know*
it was his? As good a theory as any.
He went on to chuckle about the troupe
of Russian actors who chased him from the stage
when he suggested Chekhov was, shall we say,
imperfect. They couldn't stand the thought
of all that brilliantly Russian passion,
that great heart, condemned to virtue.

For Oysters Only

Dear Anton, I have to tell you
the story of your deathbed at the spa
at Badenweiler is compelling—*Ich sterbe,*
you whisper in German. You struggle
to raise your desiccated body,
drink in one swoop a glass of champagne,
flash Olga a radiant smile, collapse
on your side, and softly breathe your last.

The perfect wisdom of your death
is too enticingly redemptive.
I have to force myself not to believe
in its romance. Instead, I try
to imagine how dopey with fatigue
the two Russian students are
when Olga pounds their door at midnight
and sends their diminishing footsteps
in search of a doctor. Instead, I try

to visualize your pale rags of lungs,
your fever raving about Japanese threats,
your soft words dissolving to gibberish,
the sound of a moth beating its wings
on an electric lamp. Instead of your
triumphant funeral, I call to mind
the train that carries your body to Moscow
in a boxcar labeled, *For Oysters Only.*

First Ascent of the Future

Accidental
for Nancy Taylor

George Eliot wrote, "It's never too late
to be who you might have been," a thought
that simmers like a sheen behind my eye
when you tell your story—For an hour
before he fell to his death, the boy
and his roommates gambled at a game
of spitting farther and still farther
from the second floor balcony. He leaned
the last inch that he wouldn't have tried
if just then the beer hadn't hit him, or if
he had been a larger man, or less afraid
of seeming queer to his friends, or more
confident of passing his course in
Victorian Novelists. So he hawked
his glob more than a foot passed the last mark
the others had made. At which point
the baseball cap that covered his pale, thin head
jerked into an arc above the railing,
and before there was time for the girls
who watched from the sidewalk to scream
or jump back, the top of his overturned skull
smashed into the edge of the concrete,
and the rest of his body flipped backwards
into the daffodils. This week, you say,
the students are looking into themselves
and carrying more weight than the chaplain
would like. Stunned by the exquisite campus,
I ask the names of flowering trees
around the lake. *This one,* you say, *is Judas,*
and the other—just as beautiful—I miss.

Chrysler for Sale

From the lucky postwar Nash
to the Olds he wrecked
the year before my mother died,
every car my father bought
was blue for the Blessed Virgin.

After the wreck, my mother
was never the same. She wouldn't set foot
in the Olds again, said it made
a funny noise. Just looking at it
brought back that night, brought back
that colored man with no insurance,
big, drunk and rude to the point of insolence.

So my father bought a steel gray Chrysler,
turbo engine, racing wheels
and vinyl top. He told her,
Don't be afraid. This car is a gift,
a miracle, just wait and see.

Propped tightly in her right front seat,
clutching her rosary beads,
my mother faced a maze of malls, ramps,
bridges, freeways and lengthy strips
until at last

the neighborhood changed
and the old apartments appeared, the sparkling
friends of long ago, friends before the war.
Look at this Chrysler! she called out.
Look at my Lee!
Look where he's taking me!

And they put down their highballs
and raised their eyes from the cards
as my father drove in his sleek steel Chrysler
through the old blue neighborhoods,
sitting erect, putting his hand on her knee
and telling her, It's all right, Peg. It's all right.

Grief

Though I had expected
to see Harry,
the Senn's retarded son
sitting on the steps
with a pipe in his mouth,
or Sherman's illicit Dodge
parked in the alley,
I came up empty.

The kitchen window
was boarded, the steps
between Senn's house
and the dirt slope
where the chicken coop
had been were crumbling,
and my grandfather's
honeysuckle hedge
had disappeared,
replaced by a cheap fence.

I walked along the side
of the inselbrick house
to Excelsior Street,
noticing how tawdry
the neighborhood was.
I stopped at Conway's gate
and dropped my hand
to the latch,
feeling irritated and sad
like a woman
who turns her head
to the window
and weeps quietly
for no reason. At that time
my mother
had been dead two months.

Crow

It's darkness that keeps me in bed
when I could walk before work, or sit
and experience quiet. There's a tale
of a man who got up for years at four
to accomplish his goal—to write a book
about silence. The rest of the day
he used the usual gears. Advertising,
I think it was. When he went on the road
they asked him to explain his muse
and he told them, *No.* This response
killed sales. Negativity—
how blessed it is to refuse! If I began
the day with time enough, I'd find
a different world—caws and tinkles,
blindness, stars, a trace of slick ice,
the cycles of crows. A world in which
I'm a part, but not apart. Abandon
desire. I've been there more than once,
but keep coming back. *No,* I say.
No. Yes, I say, *yes, yes,* as if my life
revolved like a crow from a spiny tree
to the trash, from trash to the rising sky.

Black Bugs

Nine days in the new house and you
struggle up the steps to tell me
about the black bugs in your bathroom.

Haven't you heard the word, *depression*?
Rotten soffits, sheetrock cracks, and holes
punched in the paper-thin walls.

Under the carpets the hardwood floors
are soft with moisture and speckled
like Pollocks. The sashes are stuck.

You rise like the statue of a village saint,
held aloft by children,
wavering in the heat, and on your throne

you speak of bugs, the skim of death
that dusts the splash behind your sink,
the dirt that dulls your windowsill.

I want to stick to what I am doing—
opening boxes, being afraid
of the future—not listen to you

tell me about bugs. A wet rag would do.
We must make sacrifices, dad.
The house is wrecked, we're doing what we can.

But your hands are swollen on the cane,
while today in Pittsburgh, a stranger
scrubs the traces of your history down his drain.

Guam

It's gotten so you talk about Guam
every day now, but only the letters
and loneliness. For years
I've tried to pin particulars
to your life in the war—men you lived with,
comic incidents that must have made
the barracks livable, a texture to your
boredom. Once, you talked about the mud
that made Guam stick, but never spun a yarn
about the rain. The natives? They were
dirty thieves, but now they've stripped you
to the brain. You trembled with surprise
when I asked about the town. Searching
the mud behind your rheumy eyes for *town*,
you discovered none. The only story
you remember is your teeth and the pain
of their departure. The dentist stood his ground,
though. He kept you toothless in Hawaii
two months, until the dentures sent you
to Guam. The other tales have disappeared—
if ever formed—and Guam's become
a voiceless state of being for you—like hell
or heaven is—where you've returned at last
and left me by myself. I waited too long
to redeem the war we carried on,
father and son, for fifty years. Well,
closeness, touching, matter now, not anger.
I'll make up your stories later.

Sunsets

I take him to the beach at sunset.
It's a production, pulling his body
from the front seat, half-carrying
his legs across the rocks, finding
a flat place to set his chair. Too late.
By the time we are set, sun is gone
and the last few layers of sky
are about to burn out.

                          When I was young,
I dreamed of taking him on trips,
the two of us. He wore pressed pants.
Me, a pigtail and safari hat.
We crossed a wilderness where lakes
breathe steam. We pitched our tent
in a hollow of needles
and talked about the war. *What is it, son,*
just between the two of us, you want
in life? He punched his jacket up,
stuck it behind his neck
and smiled.
When I was young, I dreamed
we arrived at the beach with never a word
about the ugliness of circumstance
and with plenty of time before sunset.
The sky was glorious, and he could stand.

Harbor Seals

for Benjamin

You think these are the same old seals
that jump and honk for food in Boston?
Or the seals that dive
for icy fish up north
in National Geographic?

Son, let me tell you a secret
about this colony of seals.
Sure they're seals, but they're also
coyotes, coyotes of the sea
who feed on the past
after its pieces break off
to a life of their own
and some of the pieces return to the sea.

The fish the seals are diving for
used to be ours. One was yours
the day you were born.
I carried one around all day
that day. Yours was fresh and complete.
Mine jumped and slapped with hope.
Of course, they weren't fish
on the day you were born. We didn't know
they would spawn and separate and leave us.

My son, you thought the parts of us
that lived in the past
just stayed where they were,
invisible and dry,
cramming the vaults of memory.
They don't, though. They spawn and grow. They seek
the sea. They feed these seals.
There is no end, no limit, to the parts of our past
that reach the ocean,
but they aren't ours anymore.

This is what I wanted you to see—how strong
the seals are, how lively the fish must be.

Migraine: A Villanelle

There never was a tumor in my head—
at least, not yet. But, even so, the pain,
that boring rod, the vomiting it fed,

came on like fate. Behind my eye, I said,
it stabs the root. But how could I explain?
For if there were no tumor in my head,

the pain must be a brand, the devil's red
encroachment, his burning kiss, the bane
of boring rod and vomiting, which fed

upon my passion and left, instead,
anxious emptiness. After which, the chain
that never bound a tumor to my head,

but held a rat whose gnawing bled
my soul of all its juice—dissolved. To claim
that boring rod and vomiting it fed

brought good is wrong, and yet they led,
when gone, to an exquisite state of pain-
lessness, this never-a-tumor-in-my-head,
nor boring rod, nor vomiting it fed.

Amber

Much of it is found by the shores
of the Baltic Sea—the strangest fact
I learned, expecting amber to be
tropical. It's the brother from Queens
who tells us about the exhibit
when Denise turns to the next mourner,
who says, *She looks just like she did
as a girl in Canarsie.* Denise
can talk the coat off a horse, always could,
and sell it for a mink. She turns death's
somberness a bit suspicious, but
generally keeps the mourning on track.

Her brother, though, is stuck in the resin
of extinction. The exhibit is worth a trip,
he says, to examine the nuance
of fossil bubbles and, mostly, to view
archaic insects and plants encased
at the moment of death. Translations
from another world—ethereal veins,
translucent wings. If you look at them
carefully, they seem to move. A friend
keeps nodding his head, nudging the wife,
*Yes, I'd like to see that. I never thought
much about amber, but I should have.*

Orpheus

Two things they taught me at the mill—
to look as if you're busy and to think
of something else, a skill I learned from Riel
who didn't believe in love, but still,

when we descended into hell, he said,
Get a rhythm going, boy, and think of chicks.
Wearing asbestos overcoats
with wooden clogs strapped to our boots

and visor helmets that made us look
like a pair of beekeepers from New Zealand,
we entered the furnace and sledged the burnt
refractory bricks with wooden mallets.

I confessed to Riel that I imagined her
behind the brick, imprisoned in the dark,
and me the Greek in hell to fetch her.
On break we sat outside the furnace mouth

nursing our thermoses. *It's not the hell of pain
she's in,* I said, *nor the hell of endless toil
like Sisyphus. Nor loneliness. It's more
her having tortured dreams of someone else.*

Riel swigged spiked ice tea and wiped his face.
And what da fuck is "sissy fuss"? My fears
were smoky, yellow, hot, and close—flesh
without forgiveness, lust untouched by grace.

Riel thought I was queer, the things I talked about,
but he liked the way I swung the mallet
and joined the union when I didn't have to.
Keep to yourself, he said. *And you'll make out.*

To hell a dozen times, but never burned.
Love conquering fire. It was a miracle
until my shift was done and I went home
from the dark river, a hundred miles from her.

Reverence for Life

At break time I sat on the loading dock
behind the rolling mill at Wheeling Steel
with a book about Albert Schweitzer
while my friends played poker. In its center
a series of photographs showed him
on the porch of a ramshackle building;
at the bench of his famous organ
which, the caption assured, was lined with lead
to allow for his music's salvation
from mildew; a shot of a muddy river
with him on the landing; and a peculiar
photograph of the helmeted doctor
examining a child's leg, while a starched,
immaculate woman stood next to him,
a buoy of duty. Unaware
of how not to pose, she looked at the camera
for validation, as if to say, *Here I am*
at the end of the earth, yet even so...
but Schweitzer paid no attention to her.
His eyes were stuck on that festering leg—
labeled, *elephantiasis*, but in those days
what good would a stare do, even his?
And so I imagined the gaze moving back
to the unnamed woman, *a European nurse,*
and her astonishment. When my break ran out,
Riel, the foreman, cuffed me across the hat.
Goddamn books, he growled. *Ain't worth shit.*

Scorpion

Arriving at sunset soaked from the road
and reeking of human chemicals,
our children neither awake nor asleep
and the heat unbearable, we took
what the bored señora said was the last
untaken room in town. On the tile
of the dripping shower, my daughter found
an humungous scorpion. *Squash it!* she cried,
an act I tried to avoid, as I knew
its slight resistance to death, the scrunch
of its carapace against my sole
would awaken a pain I hoped to forget
and so I took the children aside and said,
Scorpions are good. They eat the vermin
and even the vermin are entitled to live
until eaten. The children found my opinion
amusing. *Come on, old daddyo,*
kill it, kill it. And then my 3-year-old son
charged in with a carved baseball bat, yelling,
Take that, Geronimo! Take that! Take that!
Without a further attempt to explain
life's interconnectedness, I stepped
on that alien thing, and with a ring
of enthusiastic witnesses
cheering me around the toilet, flushed it.

Dwarf

Inside the gate, near a pair of steps that crack
the street, a voice barks up at us, *Watch out!*

In Fez, each time a convoluted lane
drops down, or turns slippery with the grime

of the density of the Middle Ages,
the same little man appears and shoos us—

first, from error; then from steaming mounds
of shit, dropped by the clicking engines

of commerce. *Attençion! Watch out!*
Half man, half head, he charges to the front

of the group and threatens the hawkers
that wheedle us with their stacked trays of daggers

and polished stones supposed to be fossils.
Beware of donkeys. I remember the rules—

Be respectful. Watch out for self-appointed guides.
Regarding photos, don't shoot, until you mime

the camera, and the woman responds,
which she won't. Silence and distance. It dawns

on me, he's back in front—the torso of a man
too close to the ground, showing me the frame

for my next shot. He touches my elbow
and points to a tray, partly in shadow,

of sweltering goat's heads—*Quick shot!*—for sale
in a butcher shop. The unreal is real,

the exotic ordinary, and the route
obvious to this self-appointed guide.

At the end of the walled city, he stands
at mock attention and, with one of his large hands,

salutes me. Of all the wonders in Fez,
that salute is the most miraculous.

The Origin of Light

For a thousand years, the nature of light
was a source of debate, a question
that split the learned, who wondered if sight
began as a beam coming in
from outside—the sun—or as a substance
generated inside, a flux we shoot
out, to bathe the world and its occupants?
Curious. I never knew of this dispute
until a patient, about a week before he died
of cancer, told me the story of Ali
al-Hasan, the philosopher who tried
staring into the sun for as long as he
could stand it. When his pain became too sharp
to stand, he understood, but it was dark.

Definitions

A firth is an estuary. A rick
means a stack in the open air,
or a pile of wood split from short logs.
As a verb, to rick is to wrench.

A bole is the trunk of a tree
in which a kestrel might perch.
A kestrel is a small falcon
known for hovering against a wind.

A chrysophase is an unusual
chalcedony, colored apple-green,
as opposed to the more common
pale blue chalcedony,

or gray, with nearly waxlike luster.
To divaricate brings together
in one word every syllable
you need to make a thing divide,

or spread apart, as with my mind.
And pomace, of course, is the pulpy
residue from which a liquid has been
pressed—precisely, like my heart.

Meeting Friends at Sidney Airport
for John and Marirose Radelet

In my mind our greetings continued all day—
from the second you pushed your valises
from Pittsburgh into the arrivals hall
until the hours you miraculously lost
came to roost, and you collapsed, astonished
that life goes on in such ordinary ways
in this other world. At odd hours I'd imagine
the first moment our eyes caught. I'd look up
from the Sydney Morning Herald and smile—
there you were, pasty with fatigue. I'd whisk you
on the wrong side of the road through dense
and exotic traffic, and ask how much rest
you were able to get on the flight.
In sum, I'd be masterful about the world,
but considerate of your needs. After a rest,
I'd walk you into National Geographic—
every tree, every sound would be a lesson
in wonderment. As it turned out, the plane
was two hours late, I had finished the paper,
and you were delayed by a machine
that wanted the contents of your lead-lined case.
The storm had strangled traffic so badly
I bungled my hard-won expertise
at getting out of jams—to start with, you scanned
the back of fuming trucks, then just looked stunned.
At some point in that industrial suburb
I ran out of cosmopolitan quips
and started to think of my own long trip,
the journey that brought me here. Like traffic
I crawl the continent's rim, imagining
its center, afraid to give in.

Crabs

If I slide the edge of Orcas Island
along your shoulder, surely I'll steer
our boat into the future—

and so I imagined that the distant
fits the familiar. Neck straight, jaw clamped,
I rowed with my back to the future
from salting the inlet with crab traps
without knowing that
an island could jump in the space of a stroke.
My arms were bent on mutiny.

That bone-like rattle at the base of the cliff
is a kingfisher. You tried to distract me
with nature, hoping I'd loosen my mind
from the task and allow the rhythm within
to take hold, but all I could hear was the slosh
and failed oars, while the kingfisher skidded
across the bay in a perfect action.

Later, as you crushed and cleaned our crabs
and tossed them into a pot, the water
was already murmuring, *Change, change.*

Decatur in Winter
for John and Lanita Wright

1.

When I first learned words
he was the Holy Ghost.
I hoped he would haunt
someone else.

When later I learned
he was Paraclete,
I imagined him tapping
a shiny floor.

Now, I think of him
as a white boat
carrying the bones of my spirit
to Decatur Island.

2.

The lodgepole pine
builds its tall trunk
to stand at attention.

The Madrona tree
curves its long neck
to look for a place.

After a few hours
I, too,
fit deeply together.

3.
I wonder what truth
the Master would have spoken
had not Lanita cried,
There are crabs on the ceiling!

4.
Three types of moss
on the island.
One is a blanket
covering an old log.
One is a deep fringe
darkening
the green blanket
covering the old log.
The third is almost
not itself, it's so much
a part of the rest.

5.
I come here in winter
to sit by myself
and read poetry aloud

The resonance of all this—
yellow grass, human voice,
fresh wood—

makes me believe
in a door
and the door is open.

First Ascent of the Future

I know what it's like up there
on the face of the future.

Your camp clings to the glacier
like a frozen thumb,
you shake with fever, you burn with chills,

your eyes play tricks, your lungs
breathe foam instead of air, you gasp
as you glimpse the beast on the ice below—

In the whiteness of your dream
you see the leopard's prey, a man like you,
who doesn't know it's a vision.

No matter how clear your mind is
down here, up there your body
comes forward to establish its claim.

Nothing, nothing is the same—your boots
are the wrong size; your fire is dead,
your canister of oxygen is empty.

What appears most plainly is the beast
and the unsuspecting man
she stalks. You strike your camp

and attempt to move your tent
to a lower slope, but it's too late—
a lancinating wind whips up

and socks the future in,
for the mountain
creates its own weather.

Cosmology
for Bill Bruehl

The woman who shot her lover's wife
will be out in a week, thanks to the victim's
campaign of forgiveness, despite the slug
still lodged in her neck. Folks take a dive
in seven stories out of eight, so the news
that redemption can be savored here
makes a splash, although celebrity—
not the tie that binds—is the driving force.

The photo of her standing by her husband,
arms-linked, on their colonial porch
drifts in—a grainy image
from the morgue of stories—as the passion
of your piece about the cosmos hits.
In our bodies' cells, you write, are bits
of atoms created by the engine
of the first exploding stars. Our birthright.

The man has gone to live in California,
discover truth and do commercials.
I suppose his wife has, too. The girl,
who was only 17 when the shooting
occurred, has found her own deep roots
in jail. Ashes to ashes. Nothing else
makes sense. But ashes slouch toward redemption,
too, from one exploding star to the next.

The Zoo

I wonder what happened to the zoo
in Scranton? Its abandoned Snake House,
the grizzly bear enclosure, the longhaired
couple of acres the dromedaries
used to cluster in, none of the occupants
is home. On our tour of loneliness,
this is the first stop my daughter takes me to,
around the back of a knoll in Scranton.
I'm surprised no one demolished the buildings
and fenced the walkways, or turned the site
to better use. If this were New York
they'd have built an amphitheater here,
but in Scranton the theaters are locked,
at least for today, and my daughter and I
are the players. Life must have been bad
for the lions or tigers that lived
in this cage with a concrete ledge at the back
to sleep on, and a fake tree trunk
that comes up from the cracked, weedy trough
at the front where they drank. *What do you think?*
I ask. Neither of us wants to think
about leaving, or to examine the taste
of regret. Instead, the apocalypse.

We kid about it—the prophetic old gibbon
who cries *Mend your ways!* And how two by two
the animals leave. The emu moves
toward the gate, shimmering in a cloud
of insects, the tentative elephant
takes a first step, a tame bear braves death
in the wilderness. But of the sense of loss
that touches her heart as well, we say nothing.
Instead, at the wreck of a concession stand,
she buys me a cone of cotton candy,
and we pass the padlocked model of a mine,
which reminds her, she says, when the time came,
some of the animals chose to stay close
to the old zoo, like the squirrels that scutter
these ruins, deep in their own designs.

Sir William Osler Remembers
His Call on Walt Whitman

I took the ferry that day and found him
in the front room of a small house
on Mickle Street, buried to his chest
in papers, magazines, and musty
brown bundles. *Push yourself a path,*
he said. *I reckon you're a friend of Bucke's.*

His famous head had aged majestically—
unkempt white beard; smooth, clear cheeks;
a fissured, geographic forehead.
His voice was pitched a shade too high,
but strong like the rest of him. Of symptoms
he said but little—remarkable

for a man of 65. For a moment
I felt that *sweet aromatic presence*
his disciples speak of…but for me, though,
it was the edge of chaos. I often wish
the man had made more of a difference
in my life, but how could I forego

restraint? Or become attached to a poet's
strong magnetic force? For a professional
like myself, his unruliness galled
and festered, though in the end I succumbed
to his charm and savored the music
of his tongue… but with restraint. I would not cross

the line between us, nor pass the gate that says,
Who enters here, abandons discipline.

Lima Bean

I have carried this lima bean
since Holy Week, a year ago.
In my pocket, the bean has not softened
nor sprouted. It is still
small, smooth and utterly different.
Like tops of monastery pews,
its curvature is pleasing.

This lima bean is alive.
A faint disappearance
of nutrients, week after week,
continues. When I touch the bean,
I am probing a deep pocket.
Inside the stony fibers,
something still is carried forward.

Sonnet for Jack

Jack Ronan Coulehan
16 May 2001

Make sure you stay in. Your warm, aqueous place
has plenty of layers of safety and such
solid good sense, facts that can't be erased
by publicists for the outside. They'll say touch,
in a many-textured world will be better
for you, and your hearing keener, and vision
more splendid—out of sight. And if you let her,
your mother—who's more than you imagine
she is—will teach you all. Innumerable
others will be there, too. But hold back. Just stay
inside where you belong, for miserable
stuff goes on out here, and there are so many ways
to screw up. But, no. An unexpected pain
arrives, and with it—us. Well, grandson, welcome.